sources from

volume 2, fascicle 2

a hurrian musical score from ugarit:

the discovery of mesopotamian music

by

marcelle duchesne-guillemin

undena publications

malibu 1984

SOURCES AND MONOGRAPHS ON THE ANCIENT NEAR EAST

Editors: Giorgio Buccellati, Marilyn Kelly-Buccellati

Assistant Editor: Patricia Oliansky

These two series make available original documents in English translation (Sources) and important studies by modern scholars (Monographs) as a contribution to the study of the history, religion, literature, art, and archaeology of the Ancient Near East. Inexpensive and flexible in format, they are meant to serve the specialist by bringing within easy reach basic publications, often in updated versions, to provide imaginative education outlets for undergraduate and graduate courses, and to reach interested segments of the educated lay audience.

SANE 2/2

a hurrian musical score from ugarit:
the discovery of mesopotamian music
by m. duchesne-guillemin

The discovery of a Babylonian musical theory, published by the author in 1963, has repeatedly been confirmed by further discoveries, notably by that of a Hurrian tablet containing a musical notation. Of this notation, three interpretations have been offered so far. This is a fourth one.

Nothing was known about Babylonian music, apart from instruments, until a Babylonian tablet (in The Museum of the University of Pennsylvania) was published by Ann Kilmer in 1960 and interpreted by the present author in 1963. It revealed the existence of a theory of the scale. This discovery created quite a stir among scholars and made it possible for an assyriologist, O. Gurney, and a musicologist, D. Wulstan, to interpret an unknown fragment in the British Museum which gives a method for passing from one mode to another, thus proving the existence of seven modes as far back as the 18th century B.C. — The next step was the publication, in 1970, of a Hurrian tablet of the 14th century B.C. found at Ugarit (Syria) containing a musical score the interpretation of which is very difficult. Three attempts have been made so far. A fourth one is offered here with a recording made at Liège in 1975 by a talented group of amateur singers specialized in ancient music. This theory is based on the assumption that polyphony never existed in the Middle East, and confirmed by a comparison with traditional Jewish psalm-songs and ancient Syro-Chaldean Christian liturgical melodies.

ISSN: 0732-6424 ISBN: 0-89003-158-4

TABLE OF CONTENTS

LIST OF FIGURES

LIST OF PLATES

PRELIMINARY REMARKS

Twenty years ago, very little was known about Mesopotamian music. Musical instruments were depicted on monuments or mentioned in texts; the famous excavations at Ur had brought to light a hoard of harps and lyres adorned with gold, silver, lapis lazuli and other semi-precious stones dating from about 2,600 B.C. (see Pl. I,1).[1] However, no music had been discovered and the existence of a music theory was not even envisaged.

Some attempt had been made to decipher a Babylonian "musical score" in 1924 by the ethnomusicologist Curt Sachs.[2] Working with a bilingual hymn on a tablet in the Berlin Museum, Sachs tried to reconstruct a scale from the tablet's first column. He did this through a statistical estimation of the frequency of syllables. The resultant melody, however, was astonishing and unacceptable. In my doctoral dissertation, *"The Musical*

---

[1] Beside the many articles scattered in encyclopedias or journals, dealing with the numerous musical instruments recovered from excavations or represented on reliefs, mosaics or paintings, the following fundamental works will give a fair idea of the subject:

Curt Sachs, *Geist und Werden der Musikinstrumente,* Berlin, 1929 (chiefly ethnological.)

Francis W. Galpin, *The Music of the Sumerians and their immediate successors the Babylonians and Assyrians,* London, 1937 (beautifully illustrated but philologically unreliable, and faulty in its restoration of the British Museum harp and of the pseudo-musical notation.)

Marcelle Guillemin and Jacques Duchesne, "Sur l'Origine asiatique de la Cithare grecque", *Antiquité classique* 4, 1935, pp. 117-124.

M. Duchesne-Guillemin, "La harpe en Asie occidentale ancienne", *Revue d'Assyriologie* 34, 1937, pp. 29-41.

Idem., "La harpe à plectre iranienne: son origine et sa diffusion", *Journal of Near Eastern Studies* 28, 1969, pp. 109-115; "Note complémentaire sur l'instrument Algar", *Journal of Near Eastern Studies* 29, 1970, pp. 200-201.

Idem., "Mésopotamie", *Dictionnaire de la Musique, Bordas,* II, Paris, 1976, pp. 597-601.

Idem., "Music in ancient Mesopotamia and Egypt", *World Archaeology* 12, 1981, pp. 287-297 and plates.

Joan Rimmer, *Ancient Musical Instruments of Western Asia in the British Museum,* London, 1969.

From the philological point of view: Henrike Hartmann, "Die Musik der sumerischen Kultur" (Dissertation), Frankfurt-am-Main, 1960 (a serious study, though little conclusive.)

The most important find was in Ur, where the royal tombs yielded the richest instruments: Leonard Woolley, *Ur Excavations* II, *The Royal Cemetery,* 2 volumes, London and New York, 1934.

Barnett in his article "New facts about musical Instruments from Ur", *Iraq* 31, 1969, pp. 96-103, insists (p. 101) on the authenticity of the lyre with rampant stag kept in the University Museum of Philadelphia (U. 123555) (see Pl. I,2), which had been questioned by Wilhelm Stauder in his book *Die Harfen und Leiern der Sumerer,* Frankfurt-am-Main, 1957, p. 48, and by his disciple H. Hartmann, *op. cit.,* pp. 22-23 (Figs. 16a-16b). But R. Barnett, after a "careful study of the photographs of the objects in the ground" and of a pair of stags in copper lying near by, is convinced that the instrument is quite distinct from the copper pair. The silver lyre is unique with its oblique yoke and its boat-shaped sounding box, but the stag on it can be compared with the animals on the Failaka seal and on relief from Tello kept in the Louvre (see Pl. II,3). Of the harp of Queen Pu-Abi in the British Museum, W. Stauder proposed a good reconstruction, which has been accepted by the specialists and carried out in the Museum.

[2] Curt Sachs, "Die Entzifferung einer babylonischen Notenschrift", *Sitzungsberichte d. Preuss. Akad. d. Wissenschaften* 18, 1924, pp. 120 ff.

Instruments of Ancient Western Asia" (Liège, 1932, unpublished[3]), I showed Sachs' position to be untenable. This judgment was later upheld by Benno Landsberger, who rejected Sachs' argument on philological grounds and proved that the syllables in question had nothing at all to do with music.[4] Landsberger's rebuttal did not prevent an English canon, Francis Galpin, proposing another interpretation of these syllables in his 1937 book on Sumerian music[5]. Errors die hard: Galpin's attempt was still accepted thirty years after in the *Encyclopédie des Musiques sacrées.*[6]

In 1960 Anne Kilmer published a mathematical tablet[7] part of which concerned musical strings. This tablet came from the ancient town of Nippur and is kept at the Museum of the University of Pennsylvania in Philadelphia.[8] Although, according to the curator Samuel Noah Kramer, the late Legrain had judged it interesting, it remained unpublished for seventy-five years. It is written in a peculiar, rather difficult type of cuneiform script, seemingly belonging to the Kassite period, i.e. about 1500 B.C. (see Pl. III,4 and interpretation in Fig. 2).

In her commentary, Kilmer wrote (p. 274):

> Column I in particular is unique in that what is preserved of this column deals with the strings of one or more musical instruments. The numbers that begin each line may or may not be coefficients; in any case their function is obscure. The first five preserved lines are arranged in the usual number-object manner of the coefficient lists, while the lines that follow appear to be elaborated, in that the numbers are "defined" before they are given: e.g. numbers 1, 5 are preceded by the names of the strings to which they apply, fore string and fifth string. What is being given, therefore, seems to be the string names together with their numbers, and their relationship to other string names, or, possibly, to certain stringed instruments. That these are string names is made clear from an unpublished tablet from Ur (U. 3011), of which the writer has been able to utilize (through Prof. Landsberger) a hand copy available by courtesy of Prof. O. R. Gurney; the obverse deals with a certain nine-stringed instrument. The consecutive numbering of strings 1 to 9 is: 1, 2, 3, 4, 5, 4, 3, 2, 1: the last four are said to be "behind." The instrument must have, therefore, either two rows of strings, one placed behind the other, or a two-part arrangement in a single row, one set of which is numbered in one direction, and the other from "behind" (see Fig. 1).

My preference, based on the non-existence of attested instruments with two rows of strings and on the fact that the animal's head represented the forepart of the instrument, as can be seen on the Ur standard (see Pl. IV,5) and on the scene with musical animals on the shell plaque from Ur (see Pl. IV,6), was to adopt the second of Kilmer's suggestions: a single row of strings,

---

[3] Except for articles extracted from it:
M. Guillemin and J. Duchesne, "Sur l'origine asiatique . . .", see above, note 1.
M. Duchesne-Guillemin, "Note sur la provenance asiatique d'un tambour égyptien", *Archäologische Mitteilungen aus Iran* 8, 1936, pp. 54-55.
Idem., "La harpe en Asie . . .", see above, note 1.
Idem., "La Musique en Egypte et en Mésopotamie anciennes", *Encyclopédie de la Pléiade, Histoire de la Musique,* I, Paris, 1960, pp. 352-362.
[4] Benno Landsberger, "Die angebliche babylonische Notenschrift. *Archiv für Orientforschung* 1, 1933, pp. 170-178.
[5] Francis Galpin, *The Music . . .*, see above, note 1.
[6] Robert Statlender, "Sumer et Babylone", *Encyclopédie des Musiques sacrées,* Paris, 1968, pp. 303-309.
[7] A. Draffkorn-Kilmer, "Two new lists of key-numbers for mathematical operations", *Orientalia* 29, 1960, pp. 273-308.
[8] C. B. S. 10996.

the last four being counted backwards. In fact, this was a succession of nine strings.

The progression of numbers, from one line to another, suggested the notation of a scale, and the fact that the progression never exceeds seven (although there were nine strings) argued for a heptatonic scale. Another fact then occurred to me that had escaped the editor's attention: the first five lines on the one hand, with the strings merely numbered, not "defined", and, on the other hand, the following ones in which the strings were both numbered and "defined" constituted two versions—one abridged the other written in full—of one and the same text. Since the tablet was damaged at both ends, only the latter part of the first version and the first part of the second version were extant. So that it was possible, by combining the two versions, to reconstruct the whole text. However, in Kilmer's edition, some of the numbers did not agree: in line 2 she read "4,3" where a comparison with line 21 led one to expect "6,3"; and in line 3 she read "3,6" instead of the "3,5" corresponding to line 22. This prompted me to ask Samuel Noah Kramer to send a photograph. Instead, he kindly brought the tablet itself to Chicago, where my husband was a visiting professor, and we examined it together with Hans Güterbock and Anne Kilmer. Following this examination, Güterbock and Kilmer provided a new edition of the tablet in *Studies in honor of B. Landsberger.*[9] In a later article[10] Kilmer declared herself "happy to say that as a result of Dr. Duchesne-Guillemin's analysis, not only were many readings improved, but we were able to restore the preceding broken section to such an extent that the progression from one to seven and again to one was firmly established."

The entire sequence of numbers on the tablet, in the unabridged version, is now as follows:

line 11: 1-5	line 18: 1-3
line 12: 7-5	line 19: 5-2
line 13: 2-6	line 20: 2-4
line 14: 1-6	line 21: 6-3
line 15: 3-7	line 22: 3-5
line 16: 2-7	line 23: 7-4
line 17: 4-1	line 24: 4-6

Fig. 2 shows the jumps from one string to another. The terms at the end of each line are given according to the latest readings, obtained by comparison with the Hurrian tablet (see below, 6.) The translations remain tentative. It will be noted that only seven of the nine strings are taken into account, and that there are three groups of five strings, two of six, four of four, and five of three. If we apply this to the oblique lyre, we may surmise that the forestrings were lower in pitch and that this scale is therefore an ascending one, unlike the scale of the Greek theoreticians.

[9] A. Draffkorn-Kilmer, "The strings of musical instruments: their names, numbers and significance", *Studies in honor of B. Landsberger,* Chicago, 1965, pp. 261-268, with an Appendix by M. Duchesne-Guillemin, "Note complémentaire sur la découverte de la gamme babylonienne", pp. 268-272.
[10] A. Draffkorn-Kilmer, "The discovery of ancient Mesopotamian Theory of Music", *Proceedings of the American Philosophical Society* 115, 1971, pp. 131-149; especially p. 134.

1. THE SCALES

What was the tonal system employed? C. Sachs had taught that all oriental music in antiquity was governed by the pentatonic system, i.e., one based on a division of the octave into five notes with no half-tone, as we find, for example, on the black keys of a piano. If we adopt this formula, however, the three jumps of five strings do not have the same amplitude, nor are they consonant.

When I tried the enharmonic system, according to some Greek traditions the most ancient, I encountered the same difficulties regarding the jumps of four strings. Thus this hypothesis, too, was discarded.

There remained a third possible solution, none other than our diatonic heptatonic system. This was already suggested by the fact that only seven out of the nine strings of the instrument occurred in the pairings of strings. This hypothesis gave a division of the octave comparable to that of the white keys of the piano. The five-string jumps were equal and consonant fifths. As a working hypothesis, I assumed that the designation of the third string as "thin" could signify "higher in pitch" and therefore sounded nearer to the fourth string, thus indicating the place of the semi-tone. There is of course a second semi-tone in the diatonic scale, that between the seventh and eighth strings, but this was left out by the theory, since it did not go beyond the seventh string.

The "thin" string was followed by the fourth, which was named after the god Ea: "Ea-made-(it)". Ea was supposed to have been the creator of the arts. The designation therefore seemed to indicate the importance of that string, just as the fourth note or string in the Greek scale, *mese*, was prominent as the basis of the tuning of the lyre. We shall return to this analogy below (see 2).

The presence of jumps of a third alternating with jumps of fourths and fifths in the Nippur-Philadelphia tablet made me think of a method of tuning, in which the sixths (1-6, 2-7) could be inversions of the thirds which corresponded to 8-6 and 9-7 and were excluded from a theory extending only to seven strings. While my first article on the theory was being printed,[11] I had a friendly exchange of letters with H. S. Powers of the University of Pennsylvania, who convinced me that the tablet was not a tuning method. My second article[12] admitted as much, but the real tuning method was to be discovered later on (see 5). 5).

In short, this first tablet gave the names of each of the three fifths, two sixths, four fourths, and five thirds included in the seven note scale and differing according to their respective positions in it. It should be noted that, as indicated by the arrows in Fig. 2, the fifths and the sixths are ascending, while the fourths are descending; as for the thirds,

---

[11] M. Duchesne-Giullemin, "Découverte d'une gamme babylonienne", *Revue de Musicologie* 49, 1963, pp. 3-17.
[12] Idem., "A l'aube de la théorie musicale: concordance de trois tablettes babyloniennes", *Revue de Musicologie* 52, 1966, pp. 147-162.

four of them are ascending while the highest goes down. This cannot be explained except as a survival of ancient gestures.

My interpretation of the Nippur-Philadelphia tablet as representing the heptatonic system was received with skepticism. Landsberger, especially, was cautious, after having refuted Sachs. However, my thesis served to draw the attention of scholars to the problem, for it incontrovertibly pointed to a musical theory which the Babylonians had worked out many centuries before the Greeks. The earliest preserved Greek theory dates to the fourth century B. C., one thousand years after the Kassite period. [13]

2. THE STRINGS

In 1965, Anne Kilmer, while examining material for inclusion in the Chicago Assyrian Dictionary, discovered on a tablet from Assur, now in Berlin (VAT 10101—see Fig. 3) seven of the names designating pairs of strings. This text was a catalogue of Assyrian hymns classified according to seven of the terms in the Philadelphia tablet, namely, those of the fourths and fifths (underlined in Fig. 2). Kilmer published this find, together with the first column of a lexical text from Ur, now in the British Museum (U. 3011—Nabnītu XXXII see Fig. 1) transcribed by Gurney, and a new edition of the Philadelphia tablet, referred to above.[14]   I also contributed to the same volume with a brief commentary,[15] and I showed the convergence of the three documents in a longer article in the *Revue de Musicologie.*[16]

The Ur tablet had provided Kilmer with a clue to the names of the strings. Now, the peculiar way of numbering the strings made me suspect that the Greeks designated the strings of the lyre in a similar way. In fact, they turned out to have counted the strings as did the Sumerians, namely from both ends.[17] Their list of strings is: *hypatē, parhypatē, lichanos, mesē, paramesē, tritē, paranētē, nētē.* Since *parhypatē* follows *hypatē,* and *paramesē* follows *mesē, paranētē* must similarly have followed *nētē.* Hence the counting of the last three strings must have begun with *nētē* and proceeded backwards: *nētē, paranētē, tritē. Tritē* thus comes third, which clinches the argument. The system can be represented as follows:

hypatē, parhypatē, lichanos, mesē, paramesē,   *tritē, paranētē, nētē*
————————————————————————>   <————————————

This is parallel to the Sumerian counting, except for one small point: while the Sumerians, on their instrument, operated with nine strings, the Greek theory was limited to the eight strings of the octave. Consequently, there was no string in the Greek system corresponding

[13] In fact, as will be seen below, p. 12, the theory dated back at least to the 21st century B.C., and the Philadelphia tablet proved to be Neo-babylonian.

[14] See above, note 9.

[15] Idem.

[16] See above, note 12.

[17] M. Duchesne-Guillemin, "Survivance orientale dans la désignation des cordes de la lyre en Grèce", *Syria* 44, 1967, pp. 233-246.

to the "fourth behind" of the Sumerians. It is notable also that the notation of "middle" in the Greek theory includes the *paramesē* (5th note), just as in the Mesopotamian names of the intervals or portions of scales *qablītu* extends from the second to the fifth string.

3. THE MODES

1968 witnessed the most important contribution to our knowledge of Babylonian musical theory in the form of a fragment also from Ur (UET VII 74—U. 7/80 see Fig. 4), found in the British Museum by its curator E. Sollberger. It was published by O. Gurney, with the help of the musicologist D. Wulstan [18] and confirmed the heptatonic principles surmised on the basis of the Philadelphia tablet. The same seven terms found on both the Philadelphia and Berlin texts here designated seven different diatonic scales and the method for passing from one to another, i.e., changing pitch, on a nine-stringed instrument. The style of writing indicated that this text dated from the 18th century B.C. The Babylonians therefore already at this early date knew seven diatonic scales, each formed of five tones and two half-tones and capable of constituting a *mode,* i.e. a fixed succession of notes as a basis for a melody.

Changing the mode was brought about by displacing the half-tones in the octave. To make this clear, we may use the white keys of the piano, starting from a C. The first half-tone is between E and F, the second one between B and C. In other words, the first half-tone will be between the 3rd and 4th notes, the second between the 7th and the 8th. If we start from D, the first half-tone will be between the 2nd and the 3rd notes, the second half-tone between the 6th and 7th. If we start from E, the first half-tone will be between the 1st and 2nd notes, the second between the 5th and 6th notes, and so on. This alters the aspect of the scale and consequently—an essential point recognized by the ancients—the *ethos* of the melody. The relations between the principal notes varied according to the mode chosen, and as in Greece, there were seven modes in Babylonia. This is why songs could be classified according to their modes, as attested in the Berlin tablet found by Anne Kilmer.

Theoretically, modulation could also be achieved by shifting the scale, either down or up, along the white key-board, so that from

C D E͡F G A B͡C   (͡ indicating the half-tone)

you get either

B͡C D E͡F G A B   and so on,

---

[18] Oliver R. Gurney, "An old Babylonian treatise on the tuning of the Harp", *Iraq* 30, 1968, pp. 229-223. In the same issue of this journal, David Wulstan, who had brilliantly collaborated with Gurney, tried to prove in another article, "The tuning of the Babylonian Harp", pp. 215-228, that the basic scale of the Nippur-Philadelphia tablet was established on the note D. But later on, after reading Kummel's article (see below, note 24), he retracted (see below, n. 27).

or   D E͡F G A B͡C D   and so on.

The latter is the process described by the Greek theoretician Ptolemy.

The Babylonians used another method, encompassing only seven strings. They had noticed that the *tritone* interval is dissonant. They called it impure. This was the interval to be altered. It is either an augmented fourth, made up of three whole tones, or a diminished fifth, made up of a half-tone, two tones and a half-tone. In order to make the fourth and fifth consonant, the dissonant fourth must be diminished into the true fourth (two tones and a half-tone), and the diminished fifth must be augmented to three tones and a half-tone.

The Babylonians distinguished two processes: tuning down and tuning up (see Fig. 5, showing the successive alterations), and treated them on the tablet in two sections separated by two signs isolated on a line: NU SÚ, a Sumerian expression (a hapax) which Gurney left untranslated and which Dr. Kilmer interpreted as "no more", probably meaning "end of this matter, now for something else".

As an example of the first process: to diminish the augmented fourth F-B, the B string (the highest string of the group) is tuned down to B flat, producing the true fourth F-B flat. To augment the diminished fifth E-B flat, the E string (the lowest of the group) is tuned down, producing the consonant fifth E flat-B flat. In the second process the augmented fourth F-B is made consonant by tuning up the lowest string of the group: F becomes F sharp. The diminished fifth F sharp-C is purified by tuning up the highest string of the group, C, to C sharp, producing the consonant fifth F sharp-C sharp.

It is clear that each process produces a definite succession of modes, one in reverse order of the other. The alterations occur in the same order as in our modern theory: B E A D G C F for the sequence of flats, and F C G D A E B for the sequence of sharps.

The instrument is originally tuned in C, although its lowest note is E. The order of strings is therefore (since there are nine strings):

E F G A B C D E F

The eighth string is always altered together with the first, or the ninth with the second, a proof that the division of the octave is heptatonic. All this was seen quite correctly by Gurney and Wulstan, but the latter wondered what the relationship was between the names chosen to designate the octave species. In my third article (1969)[19] I explained a constant in the choice of the terms designating the mode: the fourth or fifth after which the octave species was named always had its half-tone at the upper end of the group. From this observation we can deduce that the terms designated not only intervals and modes but also portions of scales, obeying a strict order: tone+tone+half-tone for the typical fourth; and tone+tone+tone+half-tone for the typical fifth.

[19] M. Duchesne-Guillemin, "La théorie babylonienne des métaboles musicales", *Revue de Musicologie* 55, 1969, pp. 3-11.

Aaron Shaffer's interesting article, "A new musical term in ancient Mesopotamian Music", *Iraq,* 43, 1981, p. 79 ff., suggests two alternative meanings for the term, Akkadian *is-sa₃-ha-ap,* Sumerian *šu₂-šu₂,* namely "overturning" or "throwing down". Musicologically, however, only the latter makes sense. And this can only support Gurney and Wulstan's excellent interpretation of the British Museum tablet. On the other hand, it is most important to note that the evidence adduced by Shaffer from the self-laudation of King Sulgi proves that the tuning method was already in use with the Sumerians as far back as the 21st century.

4. THE NAME OF THE INSTRUMENT

The British Museum fragment gives a further important fact: the name of the instrument. It is called in Sumerian ^giš^ZÀ.MÍ, a name occurring in several texts but unfortunately without any description. (^giš^ZÀ.MÍ corresponds to ^giš^ZAG.SAL in the earlier readings). This instrument is commonly thought to be a stringed instrument made of wood (this is confirmed by our fragment, since giš is the determinative for wood), but there is hesitation between lyre and harp. The lexicographic lists published by Landsberger[20] give the Babylonian equivalent: *sa-am-mu-u.* This is mentioned on several occasions and may refer to several instruments which are closely related but which differ in some particulars. It is also said to be associated with the goddess Inanna. This may help us to recognize its nature, for the instrument of the goddess is elsewhere[21] called *za-an-na-ru,* which Laroche compares with Hittite *zinar.* There is notably a *hun-zinar* "great zinar", which might recall the large Sumerian lyre-kithara which rested on the ground and continued in use after Sumerian times (cf. the Ischali terracotta in the Chicago Oriental Institute A 9361, Pl. V,7). A specimen of such an imposing instrument was found by N. Ösgüç at Inandyk. It is shown on a beautiful vase in the Ankara Museum: two musicians, their backs toward us, are seen playing together on one instrument taller than they are[22]. This great lyre, dating from the 16th century B.C., exactly resembles the great Sumerian upright lyre played in the scenes of animal-musicians found in Ur (see Pl. IV,6).

On the other hand, the lexicographical lists referred to above render ^giš^ZÀ.MÍ si-sá by *išartu.* This may be an instrument, or the name of its tuning; we know that, in the theory, it designates a certain group of strings (2-6). However, the translation of most of the technical terms is still questionable.

To sum up this philological digression, the instrument named in the British Museum fragment, ^giš^ZÀ.MÍ, is not a harp but a lyre-kithara. This interpretation, given in my 1969 article,[23] is now commonly accepted.

---

[20] *Materialien zum sumerischen Lexikon* VI, p. 122, line 44.
[21] *Ibid.* p. 119, line 43.
[22] The instrument is still unpublished; but N. Özgüç showed me a good photo.
[23] See above, note 19.

5. TUNING

In 1970, the German assyriologist H. Kümmel[24] explained satisfactorily how the instrument was tuned by alternating descending fourths and ascending fifths, a tuning later called Pythagorean. It appears from an examination of the process described in the British Museum fragment that the tuning is governed by four rules:

1) an ascending fifth and a descending fourth are used;

2) the heptachord is a limit not to be exceeded in the alternating process. Hence the alternation is interrupted on the 4th string (the Ea-string) and gives way to a succession of two descending fourths;

3) the first tuning gesture starts on the group of strings after which the mode is named and which is characterized by having the half-tone between its highest two notes;

4) the tuning ends on the tritone. In order to change to the next scale, the tritone is inflected to reach consonance.

This is the only detailed, exhaustive description known in history of the so-called Pythagorean tuning.

An important conclusion for the definition of the Pythagorean tuning is that contrary to the common opinion, in the course of the alternating process the octave is not mentioned. It is only implied when changing the pitch of the first string for the 8th, or of the second for the 9th.

Only one scale is completely governed by the alternating process; it is the scale of *nīd-qabli*, or C scale, which appears to be the basic scale underlying the theory reflected in the CBS tablet.

6. THE NOTATION

When the Hurrian tablets from Ras-Shamra were published by E. Laroche,[25] Güterbock immediately recognized in one of them (see Pl. VI,9 and 10) a slightly Hurrianized form of the musical terms used in the Philadelphia tablet (see Fig. 2). The terms, in Akkadian, were written underneath a Hurrian hymn and from this Güterbock inferred a musical score.[26]   A year later, a first attempt at interpretation was made by the musicologist Wulstan.[27] In 1973, this

---

[24] Hans M. Kümmel, "Zur Stimmung der babylonischen Harfe", *Orientalia* 39, 1970, pp. 252-263.

[25] Emmanuel Laroche, "Documents en langue hourrite provenant de Ras Shamra, II, Textes hourrites en cunéiformes syllabiques", *Ugaritica* V, 1968, pp. 462-496. The year before, I had written to Professor Jacques Chailley, of the Sorbonne, Paris: "Si les Babyloniens avaient voulu noter une mélodie, ils n'étaient pas loin d'en trouver le moyen. Et je ne désespère pas qu'on ~~hume, un jour, un texte où tous ces mots-clés seront mis pêle-mêle. Alors, on aura enfin de la musique!"

[26] Hans Güterbock, "Musical Notation in Ugarit", *Revue d'Assyriologie* 64, 1970, pp. 45-52.

[27] David Wulstan, "The earliest musical notation", *Music and Letters* 52, 1971, pp. 365-382.

was questioned by Kilmer, who produced a very different, polyphonic rendering.[28] I later refuted these two analyses and proposed instead a monodic melody, with parallels in the traditional Jewish and Syro-Chaldean Christian music.[29] The history of these various evaluations is a complex one and will, therefore, be detailed below.

6.1 Philological Background

The tablet, currently in the Damascus Museum, is made up of three fragments (R. S. 15.30 + 15.49 + 17.387), assembled by Laroche in his work under number h.6, pp. 463 and 487 (see Pl. VI,9 and Fig. 6). The writing on the tablet is divided into two parts:

1)   The four lines on the upper part of the tablet are a Hurrian hymn, the meaning of which escapes us almost entirely because of our imperfect knowledge of the language. We can recognize only a few words: the goddess Nikkal, wife of the moon-god; a gift; a heart; fathers . . .. The text is written in a manner unattested in Mesopotamia: each line, starting on the obverse side is continued around the right edge to the reverse. And the last few syllables on the first three lines on the reverse are repeated at the beginning of the following line on the obverse.

2)   Below the four lines, on the obverse, two dividing lines run across the tablet with two pairs of wedges inscribed between them. Below this are the six lines of notation consisting of the Babylonian terms, each followed by one of the numbers 1, 2, 3, 4, 5(?), and 10.

Finally, on the reverse there is a colophon which indicates the mode, *nīd qibli*, in which the song is composed, as well as the name of the composer and the scribe.[30] This mode, in Babylonian *nīd qabli* (Sumerian NIM or SUB.MURUB), is none other than that of the scale which I had reconstructed on the basis of the Philadelphia tablet, without then imagining that there were seven possible modes. As it is simply the scale of C, the pitch of each of the notes represented by the terms on the Hurrian score can be deduced from the pattern of the Philadelphia tablet (see Fig. 2).

However, three words presented problems. One, in the middle of line 5, was poorly preserved. A second word in line 7 had been read *tuppunu* by Laroche, which seemed to make some sort of sense, namely "our tablet", but musically was worthless. I, therefore, suggested to Laroche that, by slightly altering the first and third syllabic signs—the second standing equally well for *pu* or *bu*—one could recognize, under its Hurrianized form, one of the terms defined in the Nippur-Philadelphia tablet, *embūbe*. Laroche accepted the suggestion and, in fact, as appears on Kilmer's very good photo on the

---

[28] A. Kilmer, "The cult song with music from ancient Ugarit: another interpretation", *Revue d'Assyriologie* 68, 1974, pp. 69-82.

[29] M. Duchesne-Guillemin, "Les problèmes de la notation hourrite", *Revue d'Assyriologie* 69, 1975, pp. 159-173, and "Déchiffrement de la musique babylonienne", *Accademia dei Lincei*, Roma, 1977, *Quaderno 126, pp. 3-24.*

[30] In the lot of fragments published by Laroche in *Ugaritica* V (see above, note 25) there are traces of sixteen colophons, each belonging by definition to a different tablet. On five of those colophons Laroche was able to decipher the mode: it is always, curiously enough, the *nid/nat kibli* (or, as written by Kilmer, *qabli*), viz. the C-mode.

cover of *Sounds of Silence,* the correct reading, given by her, is *umbube,* a plausible Hurrian adaptation of *embūbe.*[31] About the third word, *uštamari,* see below, p. 20.

6.2 First Interpretations

As outlined above, three attempts at interpretation were made previous to my own. The English musicologist D. Wulstan, who as we know had brilliantly explained the British Museum tablet with Professor Gurney, presented his analysis, along with a recording of the music, at the 1971 Rencontre Assyriologique in Paris.[32] The digits following the musical terms indicated, in his opinion, the number of the note to be taken from the portion of the scale defined by each term. But since the number 5 appeared after a term for a four-note portion, he inverted the fourths into fifths in order to find a fifth note. This, however, did not account for the occurrence of the number 10 after a group of three notes. After this disappointing result, anyone might feel justified in taking up the problem again.

The second try was made in 1972 in Güterbock's lectures on the subject in Chicago and Germany. These unfortunately have not been published. Professor Güterbock counted the syllables of the hymn but did not succeed in making them tally with the notes. On the other hand, he believed that the syllables repeated at the beginning of three of the lines were refrains.

Anne Kilmer presented her interpretation at the International Congress of Orientalists in Paris in 1973. She divided the religious text according to the written lines, taking as refrains the last words of a line on the reverse which were repeated at the beginning of the next line on the obverse, as had Professor Güterbock. The musical terms were interpreted as chords of two notes, "dyads" or "dichords", in which the upper note is the melody while the lower one is the accompaniment. Kilmer claimed that these dichords are to be repeated the number of times indicated by the digit following each term. Since the total number of dichords thus obtained did not match the number of syllables in the hymn, she repeated the whole song, but in an inverted musical order. Moreover, she used some of the musical terms in line 5 for the music of the "refrains". Unfortunately, this does not tally. Kilmer then added a coda with music taken from line 5, singing it twice to account for the digit 10. Thus line 5, combining refrains and coda, is isolated from the song proper, which begins on line 6. This is complicated and arbitrary.

6.3 Criticism

Anne Kilmer's attempt[33] can be refuted on several grounds. For one thing, a grammatical feature pointed out by Laroche should be taken into account. The first word of a

---

[31] E. Laroche, "Etudes hourrites", *Revue d'Assyriologie* 67, 1973, pp. 119-130.
A. Kilmer, *Revue d'Assyriologie* 68, 1974, p. 73; *Sounds from Silence.* p. 12.
[32] See above, note 27.
[33] See above, note 28.

Hurrian sentence is provided with an enclitic, *al.* We can therefore divide the religious text into its sentences and determine whether the refrains occur between sentences, as we would expect. This is not the case, for we find seven sentences arranged as follows:

1) *xxxḫanuta niyaša ziwe šinute zuturiya ubugara xxḫuburni.*
2) *Tašal killa zili šipri ḫumaruḫat uwari ḫumaruḫat uwari wandanita ukuri kurkurta.*
3) *Išalla ulali kabgi allibgi širit murnušu.*
4) *Wešal tatib tišia wešal tatib tišia unuga kapšili unugat akli šamšamme xlil.*
5) *Uklal tununitax(xx)-ka kalitanil nikala kalitanil nikala.*
6) *Niḫurašal ḫana ḫanuteti.*
7) *Attayaštal atarri ḫueti ḫanuka (xxxxxxx)-aššati wewe ḫanuku.*

The repeated words occur once at the end of a sentence (sentence 5), once in the middle (sentence 2) and once at the beginning (sentence 4). (Sentences 1, 3, 6 and 7 have no refrain at all.)

The theory that these are refrains must therefore be dropped, and we must return to Laroche's suggestion to take the repeated words as catchlines.[34] Kilmer discarded Laroche's suggestion on the ground that a catchline never occurs in Babylonia between different parts of a tablet, but only between successive tablets of a series. However, the hypothesis that these are catchlines is justified by the fact that the writing goes recto-verso—an arrangement unknown in Mesopotamia. Matching the transcription (Fig. 6) with the cuneiform (Pl. VI,9), the reader may see that the repetitions could serve the function of catchlines as the musician turned the tablet over during a performance, or when rehearsing.

In addition, if we examine the musical terms, we cannot help but notice sequences of terms repeated in the same order, which must constitute musical themes. (see Figs. 6 and 7). The first of these, which we may call Theme A (line 6), is *titim išarte, zirte, šaḫri, xxte, irbute,* which recurs with the last word of line 7 and the first half of line 8. *Theme B* appears in lines 8 and 9; it is made up of a triple repetition of *šaḫri-šaššate.* Finally, *Theme C,* also made up of two expressions, *kitme-qablīte,* repeated three times, terminates the song. Such a structure, which in my opinion is of fundamental importance, escaped Kilmer's notice; for example, she interrupts Theme B after two dichords in order to introduce her so-called refrain.

An examination of Anne Kilmer's copy (Pl. VI,11) reveals three details which confirm my interpretation.

　　1)　At the beginning of the hymn two or three syllables are missing. Kilmer only counts one.

　　2)　In the first line of the musical notation there appear to be only two vertical wedges after the third word rather than three, and according to the spacing of the existing signs there is no room for a third. However, the third wedge is necessary to support Kilmer's hypothesis that the number of repetitions (3+1+?) is equal to seven, to account for the seven syllables of the refrain.

---

[34] Laroche, *Ugaritica* V, 1968, p. 464.

ILLUSTRATIONS

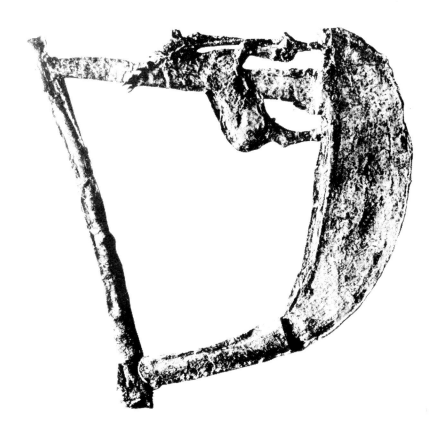

Ill. 2. Oblique silver lyre-kithara
(Courtesy of the University Museum, University of Pennsylvania)

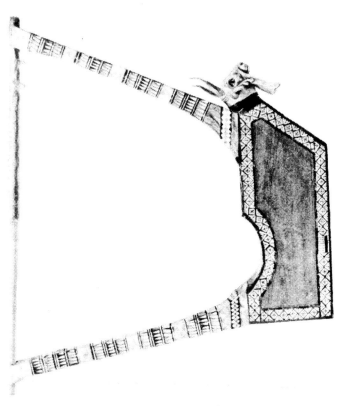

Ill. 1. Lyre-kithara from Ur
(Courtesy of the Baghdad Museum)

Ill. 3. Tello relief
(Courtesy of the Musée du Louvre)

CBS 10996	Translation of CBS 10996

Obv. col. I (at least 5 lines broken away at beginning)

⌈2⌉, ⌈4⌉		⌈SA x x⌉-tum
4, 3		SA kit-mu
3, 6		SA ti-x i-šar-tum
7, 4		sa-ti-tum
10'.	4, 6	sa-muš-šum

SA qud-mu-ú ù SA 5-šú 1, 5 SA man-ga-ri
SA 3 uḫ-ri ù SA 5-šú 7, 5 SA SAR.NÍGIN
SA ša-GE₄ ù SA 4 uḫ-ri 2, 6 SA i-šar-tum
SA qud-mu-ú ù SA 4 uḫ-ri 1, 6 SA šal-šá-tum
15'. SA 3(!)-šú SIG ù SA 3-šú uḫ-ri 3, 4 SA em-bu-bu
SA šá-GE₄ ù SA 3-šú uḫ-ri 2, 4 SA 4-tu
SA ᵈé-a-DÙ ù SA qud-mu-ú 4, 1 SA NIM.MÚRUB
SA qud-mu-ú ù SA 3-šú SIG 1, 3 SA GIŠ.NIM.MA
SA MÌN 3-šú ù SA šá-GE₄ 5, 2 SA MÚRUB-tu
20'. SA šá-GE₄ ù SA ᵈé-a-DÙ 2, 4 SA ⌈x⌉ MÚRUB-tú
SA 4 uḫ-ri ù SA 3-šú SIG 6, 3 S[A   ]
SA 3-šú SIG ù SA 5-šú ⌈3⌉, [   ]
SA 3-šú uḫ-ri ù [   ]
SA ᵈé-a-DÙ [   ]

(remainder of col. broken)

Obv. col. I (five or more lines broken)

⌈2,⌉ ⌈4⌉		....string
4, 3		" covered " string
3, 6		" ....upright " string
7, 4		" first " string
10'.	4, 6	" second(?) " string

fore string and fifth string 1, 5 " reed basket " string
third-behind string and fifth string 7, 5 .... string
second string and fourth-behind string 2, 6 " upright " string
fore string and fourth-behind string 2, 6 " third " string
15'. third thin string and third-behind string 3, 4 " flute " string
second string and third-behind string 2, 4 " fourth " string
" Ea-made(-it) " string and fore string 4, 1 .... string
fore string and third thin string 1, 3 " Elamite " string
....string and second string 5, 2 " middle " string
20'. second string and " Ea-made(-it) " string 2,4 " ....middle " string
fourth–behind string and third thin string 6, 3 [   ]
third thin string and fifth string ⌈3⌉, [   ]
third–behind string and [   ]
" Ea-made–it) " string [   ]

(remainder broken)

Ill. 4. Nippur Tablet CBS 10996

(Courtesy of the University Museum, University of Pennsylvania.
Reprinted from Anne Kilmer, "Two Lists of Key Numbers", *Orientalia* 29, 1960, pp. 278 and 281)

Ill. 5. Ur standard
(Courtesy of the Trustees of the British Museum)

Ill. 6. Shell plaque from Ur
(Courtesy of the University Museum, University of Pennsylvania)

Ill. 7.   Giant lyre-kithara from Ischali
(Courtesy of the Oriental Institute, University of Chicago)

Ill. 8.   Funerary pillar, Xanthos
(Courtesy of P. Demargne)

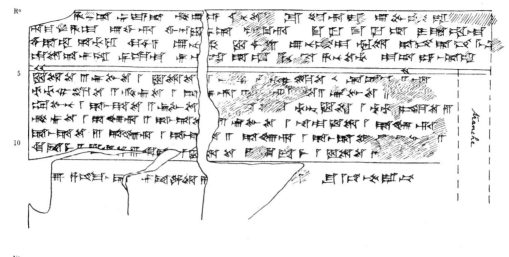

Ill. 9. Hurrian Tablet, copy by E. Laroche
(Reprinted from E. Laroche, "Documents hourrites . . .", *Ugaritica* V, 1968, p. 487)

Ill. 10. Hurrian Tablet, photographed by A. Kilmer in the Damascus Museum
(Courtesy of the Damascus Museum. Reprinted from Anne Kilmer, *Sounds from Silence*, 1976, cover)

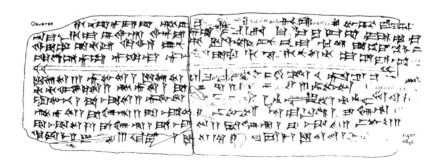

Ill. 11. Hurrian Tablet, copy by A. Kilmer
(Courtesy of Anne Kilmer. Reprinted from *Sounds from Silence*, 1976, p. 12)

3)   The restored *ša šini* "of two, double" in the middle of line 5 is essential to Kilmer's interpretation, since it suggests to her the idea of repeating the melody, the refrains and the coda in order to make the musical notation tally with the words of the hymn. However, there hardly seems to be enough room for the three syllables required by the restoration proposed. Moreover, it is difficult to accept so fundamental a reconstruction on the basis of a mutilated passage.

Kilmer's theory is also questionable from a musicological point of view. I expressed this to her in Paris and Wulstan also demurred in a review article.[35] It must be stressed that music has remained monodic in the Near East up to the present day. If it had been only a question of heterophony, which may have been known in Greek music, one would expect to find first of all among the dichords the octave, which is the most natural heterophony. However, there are no octaves. In addition, there is no example of noting together both a song and its accompaniment.

Dr. Kilmer published her interpretation in the *Revue d'Assyriologie*[36] and issued, with the assistance of Richard L. Crocker and Robert R. Brown, a record and a booklet,[37] *Sounds from Silence,* in 1976. Of the latter work, the philological and historical sections, which deal with the opening of this new area of Assyriology, are almost entirely correct: the reproduction of the three fragments which Laroche so fortunately joined is clear and the photographs of the tablet, taken at the Damascus Museum and slightly enlarged, are excellent. However, the musicological discussion is questionable, not only in the matter of polyphony but on several other grounds. For one thing, it accepts a useless hypothesis put forward by Stauder[38] who reconstructed the theory of the Philadelphia tablet as if it were meant to be demonstrated on a nine- or seven-stringed *lute*, an instrument which never existed in ancient Mesopotamia. Mesopotamian theory was based on a lyre.[39]

When Kilmer and Crocker attempted to restore the British Museum tablet, they stripped it of the stage of the process which started from the *išartu,* and began with the *qablītu*-tuning. This left only six modes in the first column, instead of seven. One wonders why the instrument should not begin with its normal tuning, that of the *išartu* in the C-scale (beginning with E). It is clear, that Kilmer and Crocker did not understand that the two methods of modulation consisted in flattening and sharpening, not in de-sharpening and sharpening. This is certain, since the method, especially in its first stage, must always start from the usual "accordatura" (Fig. 5). The two processes are described successively in the British Museum tablet.

Finally, the reconstruction of the Megiddo lyre suggested by R. Brown needs to be qualified (Fig. 8). On p. 20 of the booklet. we read:

[35] D. Wulstan, "Music from ancient Ugarit", *Revue d'Assyriologie* 68, 1974, pp. 125-128.

[36] See above, note 28.

[37] A. Draffkorn-Kilmer, Richard L. Crocker, Robert R. Brown, *Sounds from Silence,* Berkeley, 1976, in which Dr. Kilmer's hypothesis is essentially unchanged.

[38] W. Stauder, "Ein Musiktractat aus dem zweiten vorchristlichen Jahrtausend", *Festschrift W. Wiora,* Kassel, 1967, pp. 157-163.

[39] See above, n. 19.

It is impossible to determine on the basis of the Megiddo ivory whether the strings were terminated by being inserted in the top of the sounding box (in the manner of a harp), or whether they passed over a bridge (on the side toward the musician's body) and were attached to the side or underside of the sounding box. Since the latter method might have interfered with the playing of the instrument, as depicted, Brown[40] decided to insert the strings into the top of the sound box, i.e. the sound board, by means of small wooden pegs which secure the knotted strings.

I cannot see why the other method should have "interfered with the playing of the instrument" when, in fact, it is the only method attested by all the lyres which have been preserved or unambiguously represented in the ancient Near East. It is essential to the definition of the lyre that the strings run parallel to the sounding box, passing over a bridge which transmits their vibrations to the sound board, and that they be attached to the bottom of the box. This was also noted by Professor Th. J. H. Krispijn, of Leiden, Netherlands, who made a correct reconstruction of the Megiddo lyre which he demonstrated at the University of Leuven, Belgium, in 1979.

Another attempt must be mentioned which, as far as the music is concerned, entirely relies on Anne Kilmer's theory. This is the study which was submitted at the Rencontre Assyriologique in Paris in 1977 by Hans Jochen Thiel.[41] He does not offer an original musical reconstruction, but presents an investigation of the rhythmic structure of the hymn. He obtains rhythmical patterns and symmetries which seem at first sight very impressive. On closer examination, however, several objections arise.

   1)   He postulates the existence of two hymns assembled on a single tablet, in spite of which he cannot make use of all the Babylonian terms: at certain points he is short of syllables, while at others, for instance between the two songs, a note without words must be repeated as often as ten times.

   2)   To obtain his rhythmic symmetries he must alter the text. For example, he must read the four syllables *ni-ḫu-ra-šal* as three, and the three of *u-kur-ri* as one!

   3)   The stanzas of his second hymn begin with the repeated words at the end of the reverse-lines, which is a very strange place indeed for a hymn or stanza to begin.

   4)   Does the reconstructed pattern, 7-7-5-9-9, have any known parallel?

   5)   The music is strangely distributed. The second song begins with the repetition of theme A, already used in the first song. This is unlikely, even according to Thiel's own theory, since the two songs differ in their rhythmic pattern. How, then, can they use the same tune?

   6)   The author seems to have been fascinated by the digits to the extent that he neglected the differential meaning of the musical terms.

[40] Since the booklet was a collective publication, it was necessary to specify who was responsible for the reconstruction of the lyre.
[41] Hans J. Thiel, "Der Text und die Notenfolgen des Musiktextes aus Ugarit", *Studi Micenei ed Egeo-Anatolici* 18, 1977, pp. 109-136.

7)   In the latter he sees only dichords, as does Kilmer, instead of groups of notes, the only solution compatible with the absence of polyphony in the East.

6.4 A New Interpretation

My own interpretation now follows. Professor Laroche's remark on the division of the sentences by means of the enclitic suddenly shed light on the problem. Starting from his observation, I realized that the beginning of the musical themes should coincide with that of the sentences.

It was necessary to start all over again from reliable elements. The mode given by the colophon indicated the C-scale and, consequently, the place of each of the groups. They could only be portions of the scale, not dichords (polyphony) or intervals, for a series of jumps without intermediary notes would have resulted in an impossible melody. We also knew from the British Museum tablet U7/80 that the names of fourths and fifths designated portions of a scale which always had the semitone as their upper part. We were aware of the directions (see arrows in Fig. 2) in which the portions of the scale ran. The next step consisted of putting all these portions in a row without taking the digits into account (see Fig. 9). In two instances I noticed awkward intervals between them: one between *irbute* and *naat kabli,* in line 8, was an augmented fourth, a tritone which was considered impure by the Babylonian theoreticians; the other was a jump of a seventh, upper B to lower C (line 6 between *irbute* and *šaššate*), an interval which would be rather difficult for the singers to perform. I concluded that the digits following each term must serve to manage a transition between the successive portions of the scale and that they probably represented notes added to avoid dissonance. Moreover, these digits also provided more notes to match the syllables of the hymn (cf. Fig. 6).

Two problems now remained:

1)   Which additional notes were selected by the musician? Logically, they had to belong to the portion of the scale designated by the preceding term, since otherwise another term would have been used.

2)   What was their place? This depended, on the one hand, upon their number and, on the other hand, upon the necessity of avoiding dissonance. For example, number 1 could not merely be a repetition of the previous note, for this would not have changed anything to the dissonance. The solution had to be the simplest and easiest for the singers to remember; it could very well be the last-but-one note of the group. Moreover, for the digits 2, 3, 4, 5 and 10 the interval in which they had to move should not exceed the interval of a second (i.e., two contiguous notes), because if the additional notes had reached the interval of a third or more they could have been designated by one of the expressions of the Philadelphia tablet. Above all, the method had to be the same for all cases.

The interval of a second was the only one recommended by logic, simplicity and ease of remembrance. Such an interval had to be designated by a digit, since there was no term for a second in the Philadelphia tablet. In addition the digit 10, placed after the third *titim-išarte* (line 5) could now be easily interpreted as a *trill*, which the ancient Greek musicians called *teretismos.* The presence of the trill allowed us to recognize the music as melismatic, that is, ornamented, not syllabic; each syllable could be spread over several notes.

This opened up new perspectives. I approached the problem of structure in trying to make the beginnings of sentences coincide with those of the themes (Fig. 10). The first sentence, along with the first line of the notation (uncertain because of one unknown and one erased word) I temporarily left aside. The second sentence could begin on theme A, while the third one coincided with the intermediary development and the fourth began with the reentry of theme A. I was greatly encouraged when I saw that theme B coincided with sentences 5 and 6. Since the length of sentence 5 is approximately double the length of sentence 6, and since the theme is a triple repetition, it follows that sentence 6 has to tally with the final repetition of *šaḫri* (B, A, G) and *šaššate* (C, D, E, F, G, A). This was the equivalent of nine notes, while the text *'niḫurasal ḫana ḫanuteti'* has 10 syllables—a proof that the digits designated additional notes.

The trill is not an isolated ornament; the groups of sixths and their additional notes provide melismatic passages in a rhythm alternating between ternary and binary, according to the distribution of syllables. In fact, the rhythmic element is highly conjectural, since we have no idea how Hurrian was accented. However, it seems safe and fairly plausible to conclude that the beginning of each word coincided, as far as possible, with the beginning of a musical term. Sometimes two short words naturally coincide with one term and its additional notes. When a syllable is sung on a single note I give it the value of one beat; if it is extended over several notes I break it down into smaller values. The measure is free, which is usual in oriental music. The tempo is rather slow.

We are left with the first and third of the three difficult words mentioned above.[42] At the erased spot in line 5 there is room for two syllables, but not three. In searching through the list of Hurrian terms published by Laroche[43] (pp. 484-485), I found that the only disyllabic one was *ešgi* or *išgi.* Musically this hypothesis is plausible, for this term designates the C D E third, which is included in the modal fourth *nīd qibli* (F E D C).

As to the unknown word *uštamari,* we have nothing to guide us except aesthetics. It seemed to me that after a trill it was quite possible for a musical phrase to end on a long note, whether it was repeated or not. Did the Hurrians have words for single notes? They had quite a few terms of which the meaning is still unknown to us. One of these is *etamašeani,* which Laroche interprets as the Ugaritic equivalent of the string called "Ea made it" in Babylonia. Since the latter term is used in the notation it may have designated the note of the fourth string. Could we therefore say that *uštamari* designates the note of the third string? This is merely a conjecture, and I have put it between brackets in my musical transcription.

This transcription (Fig. 11) has four distinctive features:

---

[42] See above, p. 14.
[43] See above, note 25. About *etamašeani* see note 31, P. 128.

1)   It offers a *thematic structure* corresponding to the sentences of the hymn.

2)   It uses *melismata,* and because of the groups formed by the sixths and their added notes, the trill does not stand isolated.

3)   It offers word endings on contiguous notes, or *endings of the melody on seconds,* which is highly characteristic.

4)   The rhythm fluctuates between binary and ternary passages.

7. COMPARISONS WITH JEWISH AND SYRO-CHALDEAN MUSIC

The overall result compares interestingly with the traditional Jewish music which has been carefully preserved in the liturgy. The imposing corpus of Jewish songs collected by Idelsohn between 1914 and 1932 in Jewish communities of the Near East and Europe has helped a great deal in establishing this comparison.[44]   There is, among other examples, a psalm of the Babylonian Jews (Fig. 12) in which:

1)   the *ambitus* never exceeds *seven* notes, just as in the Hurrian hymn. It therefore seems to go back to a rather primitive period.

2)   The structure offers *three themes* on a continuous text. The latter cannot therefore be the cause of the musical repetitions.

3)   The grouping of the syllables produces passages which are slightly adorned on *alternate binary and ternary rhythms,* with groups of *six notes* or more, as in our hymn.

4)   There are *endings on seconds* comparable to the added notes in our tablet.

It seems reasonable to infer that the Babylonian tradition survived not only in Mesopotamia but in the whole Diaspora, as attested by other examples. The Hurrians, who had become neighbors of Israel, may have acted as intermediaries long before the captivity of the Jews in Babylon.

In the rendering of the reconstructed melody I have repeated the first phrase, on the analogy of the Jewish songs; in our case the two pairs of small angle wedges on the double horizontal dividing line may well signify this repetition. On the other hand, this first phrase was probably sung by a soloist rather than by a choir, because of the trill.[45]

---

[44] Abraham Z. Idelsohn, *Thesaurus of Oriental Hebrew Melodies,* Paris-Berlin-Jerusalem, 1914-1932. The example cited is in vol. II, *Gesänge der babylonischen Juden,* 1922, n. 95.

[45] A suggestion made to me by M. Marc Honegger, président de la Société de Musicologie de France, to whom I wish to express my gratitude.

Further points of comparison are afforded by the old Christian music of Syria. This was collected by Dom Parisot[46] at the end of the 19th century and more recently by Dom Jeannin.[47] Although this collection was made only fifty years ago, it represents the art of a small minority which clung to its tradition. It is diatonic music, often built on three themes (Fig. 13); there are also ornamented alleluias on fluctuating rhythms, with endings on second. Finally, I have found in the last part of a long composition a structure (Fig. 14) remarkably similar to theme C in the Hurrian hymn; after a short introduction, a double motif recalling the *kitme-kablite* pair is repeated three times and ends on an abridged form of the same pattern. It appears that musical patterns go down the centuries. The Gregorian chant, heir to the oriental tradition, still carries the echo of endings in seconds. I am thinking of the "Veni Creator."

The rendering recorded on the cassette was made by the male choir of the group of Maurice Triaille, Liège (Belgium). This music does not sound particularly strange to our ears. We seem instinctively to recognize it, and I think it may be considered as part of our ancestral heritage.

8. CONCLUSION

To quote Professor R. P. Winnington-Ingram, "It is really fascinating the way these documents have turned up in succession and provided a progressive illumination. And it is astonishing to find such a highly developed theory at this early date."[48] The most remarkable point is probably the fact that the Babylonian theory was based on a heptatonic system similar to ours. Babylonian influence had reached the Mediterranean coast and seems to have extended, through the Jewish and Syro-Chaldean heritage, to early medieval Europe, where it remained fundamentally unaltered until the invention of polyphony.

How did Babylonian influence affect the Greek theory? This problem must be approached with caution. With regard to musical instruments, it seems probable that the use of the lyre spread to Greece and even beyond, for it is attested in the Halstatt culture of the Iron Age. The Greeks called this instrument 'kithara.'[49] They did not doubt the oriental origin of the kithara, but they did not look further east than Asia Minor. When, in my

[46] Dom J. Parisot, *Rapport sur une mission scientifique en Turquie d'Asie*, Paris, 1899, p. 234, n. 334.
[47] Dom J. Jeannin, *Mélodies liturgiques syriennes et chaldéennes*, Paris, 1924, 2 vol. Examples cited from vol. II, p. 10, n. 13, and pp. 46-47, n. 64.
[48] In a letter dated January 24, 1969, one of many exchanged with the British specialist in Greek music.
[49] The *kithara* was the concert instrument, the one used in competitions. The Greeks had also a more simple instrument, made from a tortoise shell and the horns of an animal. They called it *lyra*. They believed it to be the more primitive type, and that they had invented it. After the Sumerian discoveries, many musicologists now believe the lyre to be a degenerate form of the kithara. Prehistoric instruments are often taller than those attested later. In Ethiopia, both types (the big *baganna* and the small *kissar*) survive.

first article,[50] I proposed to view the richly adorned Sumero-Babylonian instruments as ancestors of the *kithara,* most specialists in Greek music (though not C. Sachs and O. Gombosi) were unconvinced or hostile. The chief objection was that the animal's head present on the Sumerian lyre was absent in the Greek *kithara.* However, the Xanthos excavations have yielded a relief depicting Apollo playing a *kithara* which was adorned with a small animal on both arms (Pl. V,8). This proved a real connection with the Philadelphia Lyre Pl. I,2). The use of a small stag in the decoration of the instrument survived in Lycia as late as the 6th century B. C.[51], and, as recently put forward at the XXXth Rencontre Assyriologique, Leiden 1983, on numerous Attic vases, see M. Duchesne-Guillemin, "L'animal sur la cithare, nouvelle lumière sur l'origine sumérienne de la cithare grecque", *Orientalia J. Duchesne-Guillemin emerito oblata* (=*Acta Iranica* 23), 1984, pp. 129-142.

It now seems plausible that the Babylonian influence also included the method of playing the instrument, its tuning, the arrangement and numbering of the strings and the number of the diatonic scales. However, the Greeks were not aware of this heritage; they had their own myth about the invention of the lyre and they considered the Dorian mode to be their own national mode, just as the Babylonians thought that the *išartu* mode was the property of the land of Akkad: *akkadi ki.*[52] There is a striking similarity between the Dorian and the *išartu* modes in the arrangement of the strings, beginning with the low-pitched diatonic E. The name *mesē* and the numbering of strings from both ends argues in favor of a practical technique adopted along with the instrument. Indeed, how could an instrument have been borrowed without knowledge of the technique?

However, the Greek theoreticians based their speculations on the tetrachord and the octave, rather than on the heptachord. Although they started from the diatonic system, the Greeks appear to have reached stages which, as far as we know, were unknown to the Babylonian theoreticians. They added the chromatic and enharmonic systems to the ancient diatonic one, and distinguished not only the seven modes but also the *tonoi* (i.e., positions in absolute pitch or transposed scales). Finally, the Greek system of instrumental notation, which used letters of the alphabet in three different positions to designate each note, was probably more practical than the Babylonian system, as far as we can judge from the single preserved instance, our Hurrian hymn. We do not see, for example, why all the groups of fourths are descending and those of fifths ascending (is this perhaps a reminiscence of tuning gestures?) The Babylonian system was abandoned, as was cuneiform writing in general, perhaps for similar reasons.

My musical transcription of this hymn, in which I have tried to be logical and honest, has character and even a certain beauty. However, it remains hypothetical. Perhaps our quest is not yet at an end. Our Hurrian material contains many words which are still untranslatable and which are probably musically relevant. We must wait for further discoveries.[53]

---

[50] "Sur l'origine asiatique . . .", see above, note 1.

[51] Pierre Demargne, *Fouilles de Xanthos,* tome I, *Les Piliers funéraires,* Paris 1958, Plate XIII, relief n. 706. While this study was going through the press I found the same animal, only with its head turned back—a typical Sumerian motif—in numerous representations of kitharas on 6th century blackfigure Attic vases (cf. my paper to the Rencontre Assyriologique, Leiden 1983, to be published in *Acta Iranica* 23, 1984).

[52] See figure 3, line 45.

[53] I am very grateful to Professor Irène Simon, of Liège University, for correcting the English of a first draft of this work.

A novel interpretation of the musical cuneiform texts is offered by Raoul Vitale, "La musique suméro-accadienne, Gamme et notation musicale", *Ugarit-Forschungen,* 14, 1983, pp. 241-263. It is based on the assumption that the front part of the instrument is the one facing the musician. But this is contradicted by the presence of an animal's head, obviously marking the front and held, held, as can be seen on the Ur standard, away from the musician.

GLOSSARY

(Adapted, with due modifications, from C. Sachs, *History of Musical Instruments,* New York, 1940, and from Webster's *Dictionary.*)

Accordatura:	the tuning scheme of a stringed instrument (g d'a'e" is the usual accordatura of a violin).
ambitus:	the compass of a melody.
catch line:	a line containing a catch word.
catch word:	a word standing under the right hand side of the last line on a book page that anticipates the first word of text on the following page.
chromatic:	giving all the tones of the chromatic scale, consisting of twelve notes separated by semi-tones.
coda:	a final or concluding musical section that is formally distinct from the main structure of a composition or movement.
colophon:	an inscription usually placed at the end of a book, manuscript or tablet and usually containing facts relative to its production, such as the scribe's name.
consonant:	agreeable in sound; specifically, harmonically satisfying, as contrasted with dissonant.
diatonic:	relating to a standard scale of eight sounds to the octave without chromatic deviation. The succession of intervals is, for instance, in the C scale, as follows: tone, tone, semi-tone, tone, tone, tone, semi-tone.
diaspora:	the movement of Jews to areas outside Palestine.
dichord:	a combination of two tones sounded together.
dissonant:	disagreeable in sound, as contrasted with consonant. The second, the augmented fourth and the diminished fifth are the dissonant chords; the last two are called tritones.
enclitic:	a syllable without independent accent, attached in pronunciation to a preceding word.
enharmonic:	in ancient Greek music: relating to that genus of scale employing quarter tones.
fifth:	the musical interval embracing five diatonic degrees.
fourth:	the musical interval embracing four diatonic degrees.
harp:	a musical instrument in which the plane of the strings is perpendicular, not parallel (as it is in the lyre) to the sound board. The strings are attached to the sound board, but run vertically away from it, and not along it.
heptatonic:	composed of seven musical notes.
heterophony:	a singing or sounding of the same melody by two or more voices or instruments, usually with some modification (as in rhythm or ornamentation) by one or both of the performers. The most natural heterophonic interval is the octave, owing

to the difference in pitch between male and female voices. The Greeks admitted also the fifth and the fourth, but not the third or the sixth, which occur sometimes in modern popular oriental music.

lute: an instrument composed of a body and a neck which serves both as a handle and as a means of stretching the strings beyond the body and of stopping them at different lengths, to vary the pitch.

lyre: a stringed musical instrument made with a hollow body and two upright arms that are joined at the top by a yoke; the strings run parallel to the body or sound box, to which their vibrations are transmitted by means of a bridge. With the Greeks, the lyra was a sub-species of the kithara, with the body made from a tortoise shell.

melismatic: relating to or having melisma.

melisma: a group of notes or tones sung to one syllable in plainsong; a melodic embellishment or ornamentation.

mesē: Greek for "median". It was the basic note, the first to be tuned.

metabole: Greek for change.

mode: a musical arrangement of the diatonic notes or tones of an octave according to one of various fixed schemes of their intervals.

modulation: the act or process of changing from one tonality to another.

monody: a melody sung by one voice or sung by several voices in unison.

pentatonic: consisting of five musical tones, without any semi-tones.

pentatonic scale: a musical scale of five notes without any semi-tone, in which the octave is reached at the sixth note.

polyphony: musical composition in simultaneous and harmonizing parts or voices.

second: a musical interval embracing two diatonic degrees.

sixth: a musical interval embracing six diatonic degrees.

tetrachord: the basic unit of analysis in ancient Greek music consisting of a diatonic or disjunct series of four notes or tones with an interval of a perfect fourth between the first and last and distinguished by the relative position of the semi-tones or quarter-tones in the series.

third: a musical interval embracing three diatonic degrees.

tritē: the Greek ordinal number "third"; the third string or note, counting backwards.

tritone: a musical interval either of three whole tones (an augmented fourth) or of a semi-tone, two tones and a semi-tone (a diminished fifth). It is a dissonant interval: the Babylonians considered it impure.

The recording that accompanies this text was made at Liège in 1975 by The Ensemble Vocal Maurice Triaille.

Nabnitu XXXII column i

s a . d i	*qud-mu-u*[*m*]	fore (string)
s a . u š	*šá-mu-šu-um*	next (string)
s a . 3 s a . s i g	*šá-al-šu qa-a*[*t-nu*]	third, thin (string)
s a . 4 . t u r	*A-ba-nu-*[*ú*]	{Sum.: fourth, small / Akk.: Ea-creator
5. s a . d i . *5 (text 4)	*ḫa-am-*[*šu*]	fifth (string)
s a . 4 . a g a . g u l	*ri-bi úḫ-ri-i*[*m*]	fourth of the behind (string)
s a . 3 . a . g a . g u l	*šal-ši úḫ-ri-im*	third of the behind (string)
˹s a . 2 . a . g a˺ . g u l	*ši-ni úḫ-ri-im*	second of the behind (string)
[s a . 1] . ˹a˺ . g a . g u l . l a	*úḫ-ru-um*	the behind-one (string)
10. [9] . s a . a	9 *pi-it-nu*	nine strings
[ ] x (y)	*pi-is-mu*	. . .
[ ]	*i-šar-ti*	. . .
[ ]	[*t*]*i-*˹*tú*˺*-ur i-šar-tum*	bridge, . . .
[ ]	[*ki-i*]*t-mu*	cover
15. [ ]	[x y(z) *k*]*i-it-mu*	. . . cover
[ ]	[x y]-*um*	. . .
[ ]	[x y-*u*]*m*	. . .
(remainder of col. i broken)		

Fig. 1. U. 3011, column 1. Sumerian-Akkadian lexical text (= Nabnitu Tablet 32)
(Reprinted from Anne Draffkorn-Kilmer, "The strings of musical instruments:
their names, numbers and significance," *Studies in Honor of B. Landsberger,* 1965, p. 264)

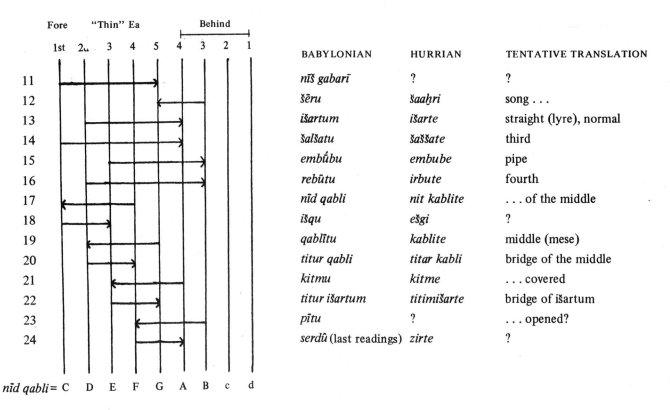

BABYLONIAN	HURRIAN	TENTATIVE TRANSLATION
nīš gabarī	?	?
šēru	*šaaḫri*	song . . .
išartum	*išarte*	straight (lyre), normal
šalšatu	*šaššate*	third
embúbu	*embube*	pipe
rebūtu	*irbute*	fourth
nīd qabli	*nit kablite*	. . . of the middle
išqu	*ešgi*	?
qablītu	*kablite*	middle (mese)
titur qabli	*titar kabli*	bridge of the middle
kitmu	*kitme*	. . . covered
titur išartum	*titimišarte*	bridge of išartum
pītu	?	. . . opened?
serdû (last readings) *zirte*		?

Fig. 2. Graphic interpretation of Tablet CBS 10996
(See also Pl. III, 4)

45	23	*irātu ša e-šìr-te Akkadî* KI *(ešìrte = išartum)*	23 love songs of the išartu (type)
46	17	*irātu ša ki-it-me*	17 love songs of the kitmu (type)
47	24	*irātu ša eb-bu-be*	24 love songs of the embūbu (type)
48	4	*irātu ša pi-i-te*	4 love songs of the pītum (type)
49	[. . .]	*irātu ša ni-it/d* MURUB *(MURUB = qablītu)*	. . . love songs of the nid qablītu (type)
50	[. . .]	*irātu ša ni-*iš* GABRI	. . . love songs of the niš gabari (type)
51	[. . .]	*irātu ša* MURUB-*te*	. . . love songs of the qablitu (type)

Fig. 3. Tablet KAR 158 VIII VAT 10101

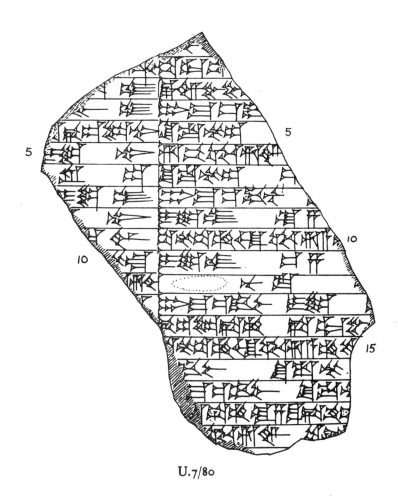

U.7/80

RIGHT COLUMN

[*šum-ma* ᵍⁱˢzā.ᴍí *pi-i-tum-ma*]

1. [*e-e*]*m-b*[*u-bu-um la za-ku*]
2. *ša-al-š*[*a-am qá-at-na-am te-ni-ma*]
3. *e-em-bu-bu-u*[*m iz/s-z/ṣa- . .*]
4. *šum-ma* ᵍⁱˢz[ā.ᴍí *e-em-bu-bu-um-ma*]
5. *ki-it-mu-um* [*la za-ku*]
6. *re-bi úḫ-ri-im* [*te-ni-ma*]
7. *ki-it-mu-um i*[*z/s-z/ṣa- . .*]
8. *šum-ma* ᵍⁱˢzā.ᴍí *k*[*i-it-mu-um-ma*]
9. *i-šar-tum la za-*[*ka-at*]
10. *ša-mu-ša-am ù úḫ-ri-a-a*[*m te-ni-ma*]
11. *i-šar-tum iz/s-z/ṣa-*[. .]
12.   ㅤ ㅤ NU   SU
13. *šum-ma* ᵍⁱˢzā.ᴍí *i-šar-t*[*um-ma*]
14. *qá-ab-li-ta-am ta-al-pu-*[*ut*]
15. *ša-mu-ša-am ù úḫ-ri-a-am te-*[*ni-ma*]
16. [ᵍⁱˢ]zā.ᴍí *ki-it-mu-*[*um-ma*]
17. [*šum*]-*ma* ᵍⁱˢzā.ᴍí *ki-it-m*[*u-um-ma*]
18. [*i-ša*]*r-ta-am la za-ku-ta-am t*[*a-al-pu-ut*]
19. [*re-bi*] *úḫ-ri-im te-n*[*i*]-*m*[*a*]
20. [ᵍⁱˢzā.ᴍí *e-em-bu-bu-um-ma*]

Fig. 4. Fragment U 7/80 (UET VII 74)
(Courtesy of the Trustees of the British Museum. Reprinted from Gurney, *Iraq* 30, 1968, pp. 229-233)

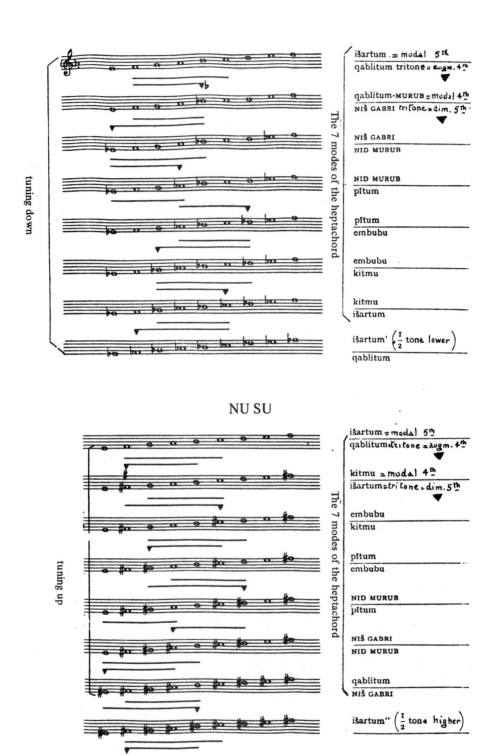

Fig. 5. Explanation of Metaboles by M. Duchene-Guillemin.
(From M. Duchesne-Guillemin, "La theorie babylonienne des metaboles
musicales," *Revue de Musicologie* LV, 1969, facing p. 8.)

Recto-verso.

1 (a) [×·×] ḫa-nu ?-ta ni-ya-ša zi-ú-e š[i ?]-nu-te zu-tu-ri-ya ú-pu-×-ra [×·×·×](b) -ur-ni
ta-ša-al ki-il-[l]a [z]i ?-li ši-i[p ?-×] ḫu-ma-ru-ḫa-at ú-wa-ri

2 (a) ḫu-ma-ru-ḫa-at ú-wa-ri wa-an-da-[n]i-ta ú ?-ku-ri ku-ur-ku-ur-ta i-ša-al-la(b) ú-la-li
kab-gi a[l]-li-×-gi ši-ri-it ? ×-[×]-nu-šu wa-ša-al ta-ti-ib ti-ši-a

3 (a) wa-ša-al ta-ti-ib ti-ši-a ú-nu-[g]a ? kap-ši-li ú-nu-ga ?-at ak-li ša-am-ša-am-me-×-(b)-li-il
uk-la-al tu-nu-ni-ta-× [×·×]-ka ka-li-ta-ni-il ni-ka-la

4 (a) ka-li-ta-ni-il ni-ka-la ni-ḫ[u ?-r]a ?-ša-al ḫa-na ḫa-nu-te-ti at-ta-ya-aš-ta-al ?(b) a-tar-
ri ḫu-e-ti ḫa-nu-ka [-a]š-ša-a-ti we-e-wɔ ḫa-nu-ku

Rᵒ 5 kab-li-te 3 ir-bu-te 1 kab-li-te 2 ? ×·×·× [ti]-ti-mi-šar-te 10 uš-ta-ma-a-ri

6 ti-ti-mi-šar-te 2 zi-ir-te 1 ša-[a]ḫ-ri 2 ×-×-te 2 ir-bu-te 2

7 em-bu-be 1 ša-aš-ša-te 2 ir-bu-te × [š]a-[aš-š]a-t[e] × ti-tar-kab-li 1 ti-ti-mi-šar-te 4

8 zi-ir-te 1 ša-aḫ-ri 2 ša-aš-ša-t[e] 4 ir-bu-te 1 na-at-kab-li 1 ša-aḫ-ri [1]

9 ša-aš-ša-te 4 ša-aḫ-ri 1 ša-aš-š[a-t]e 2 ša-aḫ-ri 1 ša-aš-ša-te 2 ir-[b]u-[te] 2

10 ki-it-me 2 kab-li-te 3 ki-it-[me] 1 kab-li-te 4 ki-it-me 1 kab-li-te 5 ?

11 [an-nu]-ú za-am-ma-aš-ša ni-it-kib-li za-[lu-zi   ] × ŠU ᵐAm-mu-ra-bi

Fig. 6. Hurrian Tablet
E. Laroche's transcription, showing text above,
musical notation underneath, with *em-bu-be* emended by M. Duchesne-Guillemin
(From E. Laroche, "Documents hourrites provenant de Ras Shamra," *Ugaritica* V, 1968, p. 487)

Fig. 7. A. Kilmer's interpretation, with musical themes A, B, C added by M. Duchesne-Guillemin
(From E. Laroche, "Documents hourrites provenant de Ras Shamra," *Ugaritica* V, 1968, p. 463)

Fig. 8. Megiddo Ivory
(From Anne Kilmer, *Sounds from Silence*, 1976, fig. 28; Bīt Enki drawing based on photo.
The Rockefeller Museum, Jerusalem)

Fig. 9. Interpretation of musical terms, with digits left out

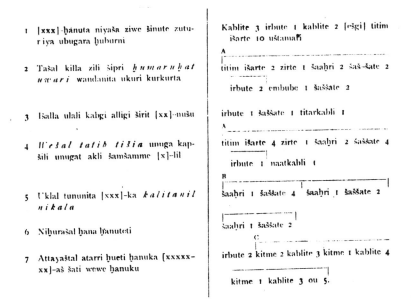

1 [xxx]-ḫanuta niyaša ziwe šinute zutu-riya ubugara ḫuburni

2 Tašal killa zili šipri *ḫumaruḫat wawari* wandanita ukuri kurkurta

3 Išalla ulali kabgi alligi širit [xx]-nušu

4 *Wešal tatiḫ tišia* unuga kap-šili unugat akli šamšamme [x]-lil

5 Uklal tununita [xxx]-ka *kalitanil nikala*

6 Niḫurašal ḫana ḫanuteti

7 Attayaštal atarri ḫueti ḫanuka [xxxxx-xx]-aš šati wewe ḫanuku

Kablite 3 irbute 1 kablite 2 [ešgi] titim išarte 10 uštamaři

A
titim išarte 2 zirte 1 šaaḫri 2 šaššate 2

irbute 2 embube 1 šaššate 2

irbute 1 šaššate 1 titarkabli 1

A
titim išarte 4 zirte 1 šaaḫri 2 šaššate 4

irbute 1 naatkabli 1

B
šaaḫri 1 šaššate 4 šaaḫri 1 šaššate 2

šaaḫri 1 šaššate 2

C
irbute 2 kitme 2 kablite 3 kitme 1 kablite 4

kitme 1 kablite 3 ou 5.

Fig. 10. Concordance of Hurrian text and musical themes on the Ras Shamra tablet.
(From M. Duchesne-Guillemin, "Déchiffrement de la musique babylonienne,"
Accademia dei Lincei, Quaderno 236, 1977, p. 15)

© M. Duchesne-Guillemin, 1976.

Fig. 11. Transcription by M. Duchesne-Guillemin
(From M. Duchesne-Guillemin, "Déchiffrement de la musique babylonienne,"
Accademia dei Lincei, Quaderno 236, 1977, p. 21)

Fig. 12. Thematic analysis of a Jewish Psalm
(Reprinted from A. Z. Idelsohn, *Gesänge der babylonischen Juden,*
Thesaurus of Oriental Hebrew Melodies, Vol. II, 1922, no. 95)

Fig. 13. Syro-Chaldean chant
(Reprinted from M. Duchesne-Guillemin, *Revue d'Assyriologie* 69, 1975, p. 172)

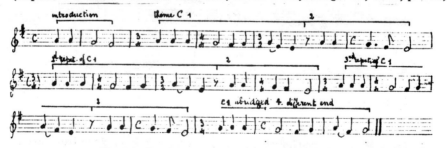

Fig. 14. Final part of a Syro-Chaldean chant
(Reprinted from M. Duchesne-Guillemin, *Revue d'Assyriologie* 69, 1975, p. 172)